FTO OR PTO?
THE SAN JOSE MODEL (SJM): CORRECTING MISCONCEPTIONS

Lisa A. Konrath, MAED
P.O. Box 12502
Tucson, AZ 85732
(520) 323-7955
lisa@lisakonrath.com

Kelly,
Keep making a
difference.
Lisa

FTO OR PTO?
THE SAN JOSE MODEL (SJM):
CORRECTING MISCONCEPTIONS

Introduction

This analysis discusses an overview of both the San Jose Model (SJM) and the Police Training Officer (PTO) models for field training post-academy new hire police officers; the recent impetus for change to "traditional" models; protections against liability; changes to the SJM; a comparative analysis of both models; additional considerations; and perpetual bias.

The intent of this analysis is to correct misconceptions brought about by the continued misapplication of the SJM Field Training and Evaluation Program, and discussed in the tenets of the PTO model. Over the years, many criminal justice entities have *adapted* the SJM *without* including essential components tantamount to its success (see below: Comparative Analysis chart, Key Elements). The result of this is that while many claim to have a SJM program, in practice they do not. These misapplications then, over the years, left uncorrected, have misled many into believing, they were, in fact, SJM based, when they *never* were. Add to this, that some even pay for and/or receive these misconceptions through so-called "SJM" training. Thus, this fact based, historical perspective and analysis is not offered to diminish the PTO model, but rather to facilitate decision making for those desiring to implement an effective program for success within their department.

This author, at the time the developer and FTO coordinator for an agency then of 350 sworn officers, joined the partnership of Michael D. Roberts, Ph.D. and Glenn F. Kaminsky (two developers of the SJM), in 1985. Since that time, her training recipients have included members of over 50 countries, 8 U.S. federal government agencies, government entities in all 50 states in the U.S., the American Society of Law Enforcement Trainers (ASLET), and 4 universities. A past president of the National Association of Field Training Officers (NAFTO) and past second vice-president of IPA (International Police Association) Region 31, the author served two terms on the Executive Board of ASLET, and earned a Masters in Adult and Continuing Education and a B.A. in Management.

Program Overviews

Both programs are, by nature, very complex. However, below is a summary of each (see Comparative Analysis chart for further).

San Jose Model (SJM) FTO (Field Training Officer Program) or FTEP (Field Training and Evaluation Program)

Essentially, the SJM is a systematic approach for training and evaluating post-academy police trainees in order to assist them in successfully performing the expectations for a patrol officer. Based on an extensive job task analysis (JTA), it offers trainees the opportunity to, under the guidance, direction and feedback of a role model officer (FTO), maximize the transfer of academic learning to actual real life, field performance.

All knowledge, skills and attitudes (KSAs) identified from the JTA are performed whether via the natural course of patrol, through experiential learning activities (ELAs), and/or discussions provided by the FTO (Trainee Task List). As a trainee progresses through this process, s/he is immediately provided specific, job-related feedback as to the quality of performance. This feedback, based on standardized evaluation guidelines (SEGs) developed from the JTA, is objective and given both verbally throughout the shift and in written form at the end of each shift (Daily Observation Reports or DORs).

Should the trainee be unable or unwilling to meet any of the expectations, and it is viewed as potentially correctable, opportunities for improvement are immediately co-developed, offered, and accompanied by further feedback. Upon successful completion of the program, graduates are deemed prepared to function in a solo patrol capacity, pending the remainder of probation. During this remainder of probation, supervisors are responsible for verifying program graduates can function successfully in a truly solo patrol capacity.

<u>PTO (Police Training Officer Program) or PTP (Police Training Program)</u>

"Developed in 2001 through a collaborative effort between the Department of Justice Community Oriented Policing Services (COPS) Office, the Police Executive Research Forum (PERF), and the Reno Police Department, the Police Training Officer (PTO) Program was designed to be a community oriented, problem-based alternative to the traditional Field Training Officer (FTO) Model."

"The PTO program is primarily focused on trainee learning. It incorporates adult learning styles, Community Oriented Policing and Problem-Based Learning philosophies, and contemporary evaluation techniques. The program structure consists of 15 weeks of training broken into 4 phases of training in which trainees apply an agency-specific Learning Matrix, complete daily journal entries to develop self-reflection and self-awareness skill, complete Coaching and Training Reports to evaluate their learning and performance, conduct learning through a Problem-Based Learning Exercise using ill-structured problems in a real life context requiring the trainee to form partnerships to solve the problem, and a Neighborhood Portfolio Exercise in which the trainee develops a detailed geographical, social and cultural understanding of his or her patrol area; everything a well- trained officer should know and do."[1]

The Impetus for Change

Publications from the Community Oriented Policing Service (COPS) in conjunction with the Police Executive Research Forum (PERF) and the President's Task Force on 21st Century Policing, 2015, identified two primary issues with current field training programs:

➤ No significant change in the traditional model for 30, or 40 years[2], especially in regards to adult learning and the need for trainees to embrace community oriented policing and problem solving, and
➤ Protection against liability.[3]

Protection Against Liability

Although here addressed in reverse order, regarding the issue of liability protection, one of the COPS documents explains:

> "The second issue police executives recognized was liability protection. Traditional FTO programs exist largely for the purpose of limiting an agency's liability due to poor training or lack of training. The design of these programs addressed the issue of liability often at the expense of effective learning opportunities."[4]

Historically, in partial response to a police involved fatal traffic accident, then Lieutenant Robert L. Allen, of San Jose, offered the Trainee Training and Management Proposal, later used as a catalyst for the SJM. He did so because he believed that it was imperative that police officers receive the highest degree of training and the most critical evaluation possible...for who else, if not police officers, had literally the "power of life and death" in our society?[5]

The liability protection cited in all of the above is more closely aligned with "failure to train" than "trainee failure to perform resulting in termination" issues. The SJM should not be included in the "traditional FTO programs" referred to above as it does *not*, by design, address "the issue of liability often at the expense of effective learning opportunities." The goal is, was, and always has been, to deliver the highest quality of training, rendering statements to the contrary inherently false.

Have some agencies altered the SJM, and rather than using feedback (yes, derived from observation and evaluation) as a vehicle for enhancing training, delivered it is as punishment? This is but one example of misapplication of the SJM, possibly resulting from poor selection and training of FTO's, inadequate supervision, and/or departmental culture, norms, and philosophies toward new hires. Thus, it is misleading to imply, as below, this type of behavior is sanctioned by the SJM:

> "As a component of the PTO program, evaluation serves primarily to support the training of new officers (*rather than as grounds for terminating underperforming trainees*) and to focus on measuring learning and development."[6] [italics added]

Further explaining the PTO model, this same COPS document also states:

> "Legal research indicates that police agencies' concern about liabilities is largely unfounded. There have been very few court cases to justify a focus on documentation and evaluation. An emphasis on effective training reaps more benefits and provides the protection against liability that agencies continue to seek. In short, this model speaks to both identified themes, incorporating contemporary COPPS concepts and guarding against liability through an emphasis on training."[7]

It remains unknown as to whether the SJM has been so successful that fewer lawsuits were initiated, but police litigation typically involves some kind of research as to what training the officer, new or veteran, completed. Handily, the SJM's continued "emphasis on effective training reaps more benefits and provides the protection against liability that agencies continue to seek" not just for the probationary officer, but   later in an officer's career by showing specifically what was taught, when and by whom.

And, yes, the SJM provides the flexibility for department's to emphasize community oriented policing if it is truly part of the culture and not just an "add on" task[8]. For example, given the SJM SEGs, is there not room to specifically provide feedback to your trainee if s/he does or does not embrace community policing while working the street?   Several categories readily lend themselves to this philosophy and are successfully applied by FTOs, such as problem solving / decision making, attitude toward the job, knowledge of department policies and procedures, self-initiated field activity, and relationships with citizens to name a few.   That is, *if* the FTO and organization *truly are* practicing the philosophy.   Or, are we faulting the SJM for an unrelated supervisory or cultural issue?

Changes to the SJM

Although the evidence shows that the SJM *has* addressed evolutionary needs and remains current, the President's Task Force on 21st Century Policing, 2015 reported:

> "5.13 Recommendation:
> The U.S. Department of Justice should support the development and implementation of improved Field Training Officer programs.
> This is critical in terms of changing officer culture. Field Training Officers impart the organizational culture to the newest members. The most common current program, known as the San Jose Model, is more than 40 years old and is not based on current research knowledge of **adult learning** modalities. In many ways it even conflicts with innovative training strategies that encourage **problem-based learning** and support **organizational procedural justice.**"[9] [**emphasis** added]

Adult Learning

Skinner's behavior modification is used as it is still a valid concept for FTOs to have in their toolbox. People resist change and, even more so, being changed. Yet, especially with a new hire, trainers are attempting to assist them in going from their "actual" to the "desired" performance. A negative, and much less successful, method of training is to make remaining in the "actual" such an uncomfortable place to be that the trainee does the "desired". Instead, the SJM coaches trainers to make the "desired" so attractive that the trainee cannot wait to achieve it.

The SJM has evolved in many ways, see specific key elements itemized and addressed further in this article, since its inception in the early 1970's. As to training concepts, it also encourages the use of various adult learning modalities, theories, techniques and methods to include, but not limited to Knowles' Principles of Adult Learning, self-directedness, experiential learning activities (ELAs), learning styles, facilitation techniques, Bloom's Taxonomy and lifelong learning.

Problem Based Learning

However, the SJM does *not* use Problem Based Learning (PBL) as defined using assigned ill-structured problems. Not that it could not, but to date, it has not. One of the main concerns over the use of time-consuming PBLs in the FTO process is that there is already barely enough time to cover all that the trainee needs to be exposed to and still respond to assigned calls for service (see SJM Clarifications Item # 12 and PTO case studies[10]). Jerry Hoover, then the recently retired Police Chief of Reno, Nevada who was a core member of the original COPS / PERF / PTO development team and both the project director and design team leader for the Reno Project, wrote that:

"PBL was de-emphasized because it tended to overshadow other equally important concepts such as adult-learning methods, Emotional Intelligence, Multiple Intelligence, and Bloom's Taxonomy. PBL is still an important concept, but can lose its effectiveness in post-academy training if it is used to the exclusion of other training strategies. Problem-based learning exercises (PBLEs) and learning activity packages (LAPs) have been decreased to accommodate the requests of PTOs and program managers who felt they took too much time from the street experience of the trainee."[11]

Agencies using the SJM are already challenged with a program duration of only 14 weeks. Yet, PBLs can produce benefits and be a valuable training tool, when used properly and in the right setting. Therefore, either the basic academy or a post-academy classroom environment seems the more appropriate place for a PBL, such as the Neighborhood Portfolio Exercise (NPE), to occur. And, it would no doubt provide applicable benefits for the FTO experience.

In fairness to the trainees, some type of written expectation for successful completion of the PBL should be on file in order that whoever the evaluator(s) may be, trainees receive specific, consistent and practical feedback as to their performance and alternatives for future considerations on the street. Policing does have acceptable rights and wrongs leading to potentially risky consequences / outcomes which, if not shared with trainees, may leave them wondering, ill-prepared, or worse, vulnerable. Our communities deserve nothing less, even at the peril of sacrificing the use of one (PBLs) best practice for training (see below: CA POST, Rubric Assessment).

Organizational Procedural Justice

The President's Task Force, as an Action item for its previously mentioned Recommendation, further suggests:

"5.13.1 Action Item: The U.S. Department of Justice should support the development of broad Field Training Program standards and training strategies that address changing police culture and **organizational procedural justice** issues that agencies can adopt and customize to local needs. A potential model for this is the Police Training Officer program developed by the COPS Office in collaboration with PERF and the Reno (Nevada) Police Department. This problem-based learning strategy used adult learning theory and problem solving tools to encourage new officers to think with a proactive mindset, enabling the identification of and solution to problems within their communities."[12] [**emphasis** added]

First, a definition for "organizational procedural justice":

1. Procedural justice is a subcomponent of organizational justice.

2. Organizational justice is essentially the perception of fairness and the reaction to those perceptions in the organizational context. In 1987, Jerald Greenberg introduced the concept of organizational justice with regard to how an employee judges the behavior of the organization and the employee's resulting attitude and behavior.[13]

3. Procedural justice is defined as the fairness of the processes that lead to outcomes. When individuals feel that they have a voice in the process or that the process involves characteristics such as consistency, accuracy, ethicality, and lack of bias then procedural justice is enhanced.[14]

Therefore, this Task Force Action Item appears connected to when Greenberg and coauthor Folger, in 1985, argued that procedural rules could be used to make performance evaluations fairer by giving employees input into the appraisal process, allowing them to complete self-appraisals, and improving record keeping procedures.[15]

The Task Force, in citing the PTO model, either overlooked or disregarded that the SJM has for many years "supported the development of broad Field Training Program standards and training strategies that address changing police culture and organizational procedural justice issues that agencies can adopt and customize to local needs." Previously addressed in this article are the SEGs which have evolved as practitioners of the SJM identified recommendations for change (some may remember 29 performance standards, others are more familiar with 31-34 of them) and innovative training strategies. The PTO model is touted in several places as being flexible[16], leaving one to wonder if the SJM is not. Yet these are but two major examples of the flexibility of the SJM as well. Additionally, the SJM has for many years recommended that FTOs make frequent use of trainee self-evaluations for training purposes, thus creating opportunities for the trainee to 1) better direct their progress and 2) self-identify what areas s/he believes are strengths and/or needing further practice. This can be accomplished either by using the SEGs and a DOR form or simply writing a narrative. It is then reviewed and discussed with the FTO; an action plan developed together, if indicated; and placed in the trainee's permanent training file, along with any account written by the FTO.

One other note from the President's Task Force:

> 5.13.2 Action Item: The U.S. Department of Justice should provide funding to incentivize agencies to update their Field Training Programs in accordance with the new standards.[17]

As both the SJM and PTO are in accordance with the "new" standards, agencies desiring to use either program would benefit from receiving funding, thus offering FTO program users to update (or correctly align) their implementation of the SJM.

The following Comparative Analysis chart is offered as a graphic depiction of the components of both the SJM and PTO models. Depicted and explained are the previously referred to components, or Key Elements, which lend themselves to program success. They are categorized by Essential, Important and Helpful. Again, the 'essential' Key Elements:

> "must be included as formatted or the program will inevitably fail." Elements identified as 'important but subject to modification' are necessary to program operation and success but may be modified to fit departmental needs, type, personnel, budget, and the like."[18]

In determining to what extent an agency has a SJM based program (or not!), *these* are the factors to be weighed.

SJM/FTO AND PTO: A COMPARATIVE ANALYSIS

ITEM #	PROGRAM STRUCTURE / KEY ELEMENTS*[19]	SAN JOSE MODEL FTO[+]	POLICE TRAINING OFFICER / (PTO)[20]
	ESSENTIAL (to program success)		
1	Commitment of the Chief Executive	Unqualified, most critical.	Same
2	Validity	The program tests that which it purports to test, as based on a Job Task Analysis (JTA), using Standardized Evaluation Guidelines (SEGs) and multiple forms of feedback documents: Daily Observation Reports (DORs), Supervisors Weekly Reports (SWRs), etc. Satisfies EEOC 1607.5a need for "content validity".[21]	Training criteria is based on job task analysis and contemporary policing philosophy (COPPS, PBL). Training process evaluated by Board of Evaluators.

---

* While primarily extracted from Kaminsky's book, the Key Elements are categorized by criticality to program success and numbered for further discussion.

[+] Correct data, several of which were misrepresented in *Police Training Officer (PTO) Manual*, p. 156-157.

16

SJM / FTO AND PTO: A COMPARATIVE ANALYSIS		
ITEM #	PROGRAM STRUCTURE / KEY ELEMENTS*	SAN JOSE MODEL FTO+	POLICE TRAINING OFFICER / (PTO)
ESSENTIAL (to program success)		
3	Reliability	The program tests on a consistent basis in that the Key Elements are applied consistently for all trainees.	Reliability enhanced by continuity of training and evaluation, commitment of the PTO and adult learner, and independent evaluators.
4	Managing the Program	FTO Coordinator reports directly to Chief Executive, or designee, who has direct authority to carry out a termination. Others are excluded.	Mid-manager reports to Patrol Division head. Others are excluded.

---

* While primarily extracted from Kaminsky's book, the Key Elements are categorized by criticality to program success and numbered for further discussion.

+ Correct data, several of which were misrepresented in *Police Training Officer (PTO) Manual*, p. 156-157.

SJM / FTO AND PTO: A COMPARATIVE ANALYSIS

ITEM #	PROGRAM STRUCTURE / KEY ELEMENTS*	SAN JOSE MODEL FTO+	POLICE TRAINING OFFICER / (PTO)
		ESSENTIAL (to program success)	
5	FTO Selection	Volunteers desired. Application; Oral Board Interview; supervisor's recommendation; experience as instructor, coach, mentor, leader, and/or supervisor; job performance and discipline records reviewed; police experience; positive role model; good communications skills. Other factors (such as proven COP skills) may be added as desired by the user agencies.	Police Training Officers (PTOs) and Police Training Evaluators (PTEs) selected based upon community skills, problem-solving skills, commitment to COPPS, knowledge of resources, interest in adult learning techniques, prior training and operational experience.

* While primarily extracted from Kaminsky's book, the Key Elements are categorized by criticality to program success and numbered for further discussion.

+ Correct data, several of which were misrepresented in *Police Training Officer (PTO) Manual*, p. 156-157.

SJM/FTO AND PTO: A COMPARATIVE ANALYSIS

ITEM #	PROGRAM STRUCTURE / KEY ELEMENTS*	SAN JOSE MODEL FTO+	POLICE TRAINING OFFICER / (PTO)
		ESSENTIAL (to program success)	
6	Training Program Personnel	40 hour course for FTOs emphasizing program key elements; adult learning principles and strategies; effective communication, coaching, and feedback; role modeling and ethics; SEGs, application and consistency; liability; supervision and leadership. Similar training for supervisory personnel. Available specialized training for coordinators (FTOC) and command personnel. Suggested FTO advanced, refresher and update training available.	40-hour course emphasizing PBL, COPPS, adult learning, program structure application and evaluation, liability, leadership, ethics. Similar training for supervisory and command personnel.

* While primarily extracted from Kaminsky's book, the Key Elements are categorized by criticality to program success and numbered for further discussion.
+ Correct data, several of which were misrepresented in *Police Training Officer (PTO) Manual*, p. 156-157.

SJM/FTO AND PTO: A COMPARATIVE ANALYSIS

ITEM #	PROGRAM STRUCTURE / KEY ELEMENTS*	SAN JOSE MODEL FTO+	POLICE TRAINING OFFICER / (PTO)
		ESSENTIAL (to program success)	
7	**Supervisory & Management Review**	Essential to ensure validity / standards, reliability / consistency and objectivity. FTO's actual field supv. (FTS) performing field visits, observations, ride-a-longs, Weekly Reports (SWRs), Bi-Weekly Meetings, and Remedial Training assistance. FTOC's active involvement, observation, assistance, and liaison w/ Academy.	Essential to ensure objectivity and standardization, plus Board of Evaluators (BOE) Weekly supervisor meetings Bi-weekly PTO meetings

---

* While primarily extracted from Kaminsky's book, the Key Elements are categorized by criticality to program success and numbered for further discussion.
+ Correct data, several of which were misrepresented in *Police Training Officer (PTO) Manual*, p. 156-157.

20

SJM / FTO AND PTO: A COMPARATIVE ANALYSIS		
ITEM #	**PROGRAM STRUCTURE / KEY ELEMENTS***	**SAN JOSE MODEL FTO[+]**	**POLICE TRAINING OFFICER / (PTO)**
ESSENTIAL (to program success)		
8	**Trainee Task List**	Planned progressive complexity training, which ensures coverage of *all* JTA identified KSAs for successful performance as a solo patrol officer. Broken into week-by-week segments so as not to overload the trainee nor FTO in any given week.	Learning matrix in trainee manual, consisting of Core Competencies that allow for flexibility in learning opportunities.
9	**Training Extensions**	Yes, only if problem(s) is deemed as correctable / remediable. Trainees help FTO, FTS and FTOC with problem identification, root causes, and recommended solutions.	Program is flexible and includes remedial training as integral component. *Failing forward* concept is central to training philosophy.

---

* While primarily extracted from Kaminsky's book, the Key Elements are categorized by criticality to program success and numbered for further discussion.
[+] Correct data, several of which were misrepresented in *Police Training Officer (PTO) Manual*, p. 156-157.

	SJM / FTO AND PTO: A COMPARATIVE ANALYSIS	
ITEM #	PROGRAM STRUCTURE / KEY ELEMENTS*	SAN JOSE MODEL FTO[+]	POLICE TRAINING OFFICER / (PTO)
	ESSENTIAL (to program success)		
10	"Limbo" Period(s)	Phase 1, first 2 weeks of program. Depending upon trainee, 1st week may be virtual ride along. 2nd introduces training and feedback. No evaluation in Limbo. Some depts. use Day 1 of Phases 2 and 3 as Limbo as well, since trainee just switched to next FTO, allowing for adjustment to new training environment.	First week of program is the Integration Phase, which prepares the trainee for the program.

---

* While primarily extracted from Kaminsky's book, the Key Elements are categorized by criticality to program success and numbered for further discussion.

[+] Correct data, several of which were misrepresented in *Police Training Officer (PTO) Manual*, p. 156-157.

	SJM / FTO AND PTO: A COMPARATIVE ANALYSIS	
ITEM #	PROGRAM STRUCTURE / KEY ELEMENTS*	SAN JOSE MODEL FTO[+]	POLICE TRAINING OFFICER / (PTO)
	ESSENTIAL (to program success)		
11	Trainee Orientation to Program	Prior to program start, familiarization with program is encouraged in academy or post-academy local training. If not, FTOC and/or FTO responsible for this. Topics include: program structure and logistics, learning opportunities, roles and responsibilities, expectations (SEGs) for participation and successful completion, and agency-specific components.	Before entering the PTO program, familiarization with the program may take place in the academy or in post-academy local training. Topics include: Steps and philosophies, introduce trainees to the PTO program, introduce Learning Activity Packages (LAPs), and agency-specific components.

---

* While primarily extracted from Kaminsky's book, the Key Elements are categorized by criticality to program success and numbered for further discussion.

+ Correct data, several of which were misrepresented in *Police Training Officer (PTO) Manual*, p. 156-157.

SJM / FTO AND PTO:
A COMPARATIVE ANALYSIS

ITEM #	PROGRAM STRUCTURE / KEY ELEMENTS*	SAN JOSE MODEL FTO[+]	POLICE TRAINING OFFICER / (PTO)
		ESSENTIAL (to program success)	
12	**Deployment Status of Trainee**	Never assigned beyond control of FTO; call requiring 2 officers results in 2nd unit dispatched.	Same
13	**Program Duration**	14 Weeks: 2 weeks Limbo + training 10 weeks training and evaluation 2 weeks quasi-solo "evaluation only" Training Extensions, at any appropriate point in the program, may lengthen overall duration.	15 Weeks: 1 week integration 12 weeks training 2 weeks evaluation

---

* While primarily extracted from Kaminsky's book, the Key Elements are categorized by criticality to program success and numbered for further discussion.

[+] Correct data, several of which were misrepresented in *Police Training Officer (PTO) Manual*, p. 156-157.

SJM / FTO AND PTO: A COMPARATIVE ANALYSIS

ITEM #	PROGRAM STRUCTURE / KEY ELEMENTS*	SAN JOSE MODEL FTO+	POLICE TRAINING OFFICER / (PTO)
		ESSENTIAL (to program success)	
14	**Rotation Between FTOs**	14 week program 1st Phase 2nd Phase 3rd Phase 4th Phase (2)+2 4 4 2 1st FTO 2nd FTO 3rd FTO back to 1st FTO	15 week program <u>Integration AB Mid-Eval CD Fnl Eval</u> 1 6 1 6 1 PTO PTO PTE PTO PTE

---

* While primarily extracted from Kaminsky's book, the Key Elements are categorized by criticality to program success and numbered for further discussion.

+ Correct data, several of which were misrepresented in *Police Training Officer (PTO) Manual,* p. 156-157.

SJM/FTO AND PTO: A COMPARATIVE ANALYSIS

ITEM #	PROGRAM STRUCTURE / KEY ELEMENTS*	SAN JOSE MODEL FTO+	POLICE TRAINING OFFICER / (PTO)
ESSENTIAL (to program success)			
15	**Multiple Levels and Methods of Performance Evaluation**	Field performance; experiential learning activities (ELAs); Standardized Evaluation Guidelines (SEGs) based on Job Task Analysis (JTA) and used for 1) Daily Observation Reports (DORs) by FTO, 2) self-evaluations by trainees, 3) Supervisors Weekly Reports (SWRs), 4) Bi-Weekly Reports, 5) End-of-Phase Reports, 6) Trainee Task List, 7) Weekly Tests, and 8) Remedial Training Worksheets.	Multiple levels and methods for application of training include daily journal entry, weekly Coaching and Training Reports, PBLEs, NPE, learning matrix, evaluation phases, and BOE.

* While primarily extracted from Kaminsky's book, the Key Elements are categorized by criticality to program success and numbered for further discussion.

+ Correct data, several of which were misrepresented in *Police Training Officer (PTO) Manual*, p. 156-157.

SJM / FTO AND PTO:
A COMPARATIVE ANALYSIS

ITEM #	PROGRAM STRUCTURE / KEY ELEMENTS*	SAN JOSE MODEL FTO[+]	POLICE TRAINING OFFICER / (PTO)
	ESSENTIAL (to program success)		
16	Rating Frequency	Using the Standardized Evaluation Guidelines (SEGs), daily (DOR), other than during Limbo; weekly (SWR) by the immediate field supervisor (FTS).	Weekly Coaching and Training Reports by the trainee and the PTO, Mid-Term and Final Evaluations, Problem-Based Learning Exercises, Neighborhood Portfolio Exercise.
17	Evaluation Only Phase	Phase 4, last two weeks of program. Evaluation is the primary purpose, but learning, as always, continues. Feedback during and following each activity.	1-week Mid-Term Evaluation and 1-week Final Evaluation completed by independent evaluator. Evaluation is the primary purpose, but learning continues.

---

* While primarily extracted from Kaminsky's book, the Key Elements are categorized by criticality to program success and numbered for further discussion.

[+] Correct data, several of which were misrepresented in *Police Training Officer (PTO) Manual*, p. 156-157.

SJM/FTO AND PTO: A COMPARATIVE ANALYSIS

ITEM #	PROGRAM STRUCTURE / KEY ELEMENTS*	SAN JOSE MODEL FTO+	POLICE TRAINING OFFICER / (PTO)
	ESSENTIAL (to program success)		
18	Functional Termination Authority	Recommendation comes from the FTO, based upon input from the trainee, SEGs, DORs, SWRs, remedial strategies, fellow FTOs, FTS, FTOC and Bi-Weekly Meetings.	Vested in PTO, PTE, Board of Evaluators, and Program Coordinator.
19	Location of Program Control	Typically Patrol Division, but can be from Training Division.	Patrol Division
20	Compensation & Recognition	Amount, frequency and duration vary by agency.	Subject to local requirements.

* While primarily extracted from Kaminsky's book, the Key Elements are categorized by criticality to program success and numbered for further discussion.

+ Correct data, several of which were misrepresented in *Police Training Officer (PTO) Manual*, p. 156-157.

SJM / FTO AND PTO:
A COMPARATIVE ANALYSIS

ITEM #	PROGRAM STRUCTURE / KEY ELEMENTS*	SAN JOSE MODEL FTO+	POLICE TRAINING OFFICER /(PTO)
		ESSENTIAL (to program success)	
21	**Other Program Participants**	Others need to be either trained to the program or possess a working knowledge of it, thus avoiding philosophical and decision conflicts. Valuable input might come from Training and / or Academy personnel, Human Resources, Department Psychologist, or others as needed.	Patrol Division head, Training Manager, others as needed.

* While primarily extracted from Kaminsky's book, the Key Elements are categorized by criticality to program success and numbered for further discussion.

+ Correct data, several of which were misrepresented in *Police Training Officer (PTO) Manual*, p. 156-157.

SJM / FTO AND PTO: A COMPARATIVE ANALYSIS

ITEM #	PROGRAM STRUCTURE/ KEY ELEMENTS*	SAN JOSE MODEL FTO+	POLICE TRAINING OFFICER / (PTO)
IMPORTANT (necessary to program operation/success, but may be modified to fit dept.)			
22	Rotation of Assignments/Geographic	Initially, a "life-laboratory" in San Jose in the one Patrol District was used. Now varies by agency response needs and FTO deployment, but should provide all trainees exposure in a consistent manner which maximizes the learning experience.	This model encourages geographic accountability facilitated by patrol area assignment and Neighborhood Portfolio Exercises.

---

* While primarily extracted from Kaminsky's book, the Key Elements are categorized by criticality to program success and numbered for further discussion.

+ Correct data, several of which were misrepresented in *Police Training Officer (PTO) Manual*, p. 156-157.

SJM / FTO AND PTO: A COMPARATIVE ANALYSIS

ITEM #	PROGRAM STRUCTURE / KEY ELEMENTS*	SAN JOSE MODEL FTO+	POLICE TRAINING OFFICER / (PTO)
	IMPORTANT (necessary to program operation / success, but may be modified to fit dept.)		
23	**Rotation of Shifts**	Rotated for exposure to cross-section of service demands, citizens, and community. Varies by agency, but should provide all trainees exposure in a consistent manner which maximizes the "true to real life" learning experience.	Suggests trainees remain on day shift and swing shift as problem-solving resources are more available, activity generally higher – leading to more training opportunities.
24	**Post Academy Classroom Training**	In-house Academy following graduation from regional training center, plus FTO program orientation.	In-house Academy following graduation from regional training center, plus problem-based learning (PBL) orientation.

---

* While primarily extracted from Kaminsky's book, the Key Elements are categorized by criticality to program success and numbered for further discussion.

+ Correct data, several of which were misrepresented in *Police Training Officer (PTO) Manual*, p. 156-157.

SJM / FTO AND PTO:
A COMPARATIVE ANALYSIS

IMPORTANT (necessary to program operation/success, but may be modified to fit dept.)

ITEM #	PROGRAM STRUCTURE / KEY ELEMENTS*	SAN JOSE MODEL FTO+	POLICE TRAINING OFFICER / (PTO)
25	Bi-Weekly & Periodic Evaluation Sessions	Meeting of FTOs, FTSs and FTOC to receive updates; exchange trainee progress and training strategies and methods; and ensure consistency in application of evaluation and feedback. 10-plan and team policing approach allows for overlap shift and minimal overtime expense.	10-plan and team policing approach allows for overlap shift and minimal overtime expense.

---

* While primarily extracted from Kaminsky's book, the Key Elements are categorized by criticality to program success and numbered for further discussion.

+ Correct data, several of which were misrepresented in *Police Training Officer (PTO) Manual*, p. 156-157.

SJM / FTO AND PTO: A COMPARATIVE ANALYSIS

ITEM #	PROGRAM STRUCTURE / KEY ELEMENTS*	SAN JOSE MODEL FTO[+]	POLICE TRAINING OFFICER / (PTO)
	IMPORTANT (necessary to program operation / success, but may be modified to fit dept.)		
26	Evaluating the FTO & Program	Ongoing by FTO self-evaluation, by trainee at end of each rotation, ongoing by field supervisors (FTSs) and at end of each cycle, ongoing by FTOC, ongoing by fellow FTOs, at Bi-Weekly Meetings, and at "End of Probation Board".	Conducted by PTO supervisor, BOE, and trainee.

---

* While primarily extracted from Kaminsky's book, the Key Elements are categorized by criticality to program success and numbered for further discussion.
[+] Correct data, several of which were misrepresented in *Police Training Officer (PTO) Manual*, p. 156-157.

SJM / FTO AND PTO:
A COMPARATIVE ANALYSIS

HELPFUL (add improvement to program functionality)

ITEM #	PROGRAM STRUCTURE / KEY ELEMENTS*	SAN JOSE MODEL FTO+	POLICE TRAINING OFFICER / (PTO)
27	Periodic Objective Tests	In addition to the ongoing opportunities for performance feedback "on-the-job", augmented by experiential learning activities (ELAs), standardized weekly tests may be used to reinforce previous week's material from Training Task List.	Ongoing weekly Coaching and Training Reports, Problem-Based Learning Exercises, Mid-Term & Final Evaluations.
28	Accreditation Standards	San Jose Model, used as the foundation for CALEA, far exceeds the standards.	Exceeds accreditation standards.

---

* While primarily extracted from Kaminsky's book, the Key Elements are categorized by criticality to program success and numbered for further discussion.

+ Correct data, several of which were misrepresented in *Police Training Officer (PTO) Manual*, p. 156-157.

The following items, listed numerically in the above chart, require elaboration due to their complexity and/or relevance to this discussion.

Item 8: Trainee Task List

If the Trainee and FTO encounter a task which is programmatically listed in a different week than a field opportunity provides, depending on the trainee's progression and level of involvement, the FTO may elect to "sign-off" the trainee in said task. However, care should be taken in doing so as most trainees would not be equipped to thoroughly handle a major incident in the earlier weeks of their training.

Item 9: Training Extensions

Agencies struggle with misconceptions and incorrect application of this key element. First, extensions may occur anytime if a problem is viewed as remediable. It was never part of the SJM to wait until just before the quasi-solo phase to offer corrective training extensions. If a problem is significant enough to distract the trainee from learning and perfecting other performance tasks, then an extension should be considered immediately. When building a house, if there is a major crack in the foundation, repairs to the foundation must occur prior to putting up the walls, installing plumbing and electricity, etc. The imminent timing for training extensions is the same. Extensions have been referred to as "unplugs" or "holdovers" as it will increase that trainee's program duration.

These extensions are different from day-to-day remedial (corrective, additional) training which occurs throughout the shift as needed. In these cases, the "foundation" does not have a major crack, rather a minor one(s) which can be addressed without inhibiting further progression.

The first step must use trainee input and previously documented attempts to correctly identify the "problem", not just symptoms or overall categories. Ex.: not Report Writing, rather inability to spell, or read and write the English language, or write chronologically, etc. Next, analyze if the problem is viewed as remediable given its nature, agency resources, etc. Using trainee input, 1) identify alternative methods and ideas for acquiring the correct performance; 2) assess which is considered to have the highest likelihood of success; and 3) consider the feasibility for the agency to implement the training plan. The questions should be asked, "Would the department, or has it in the past, do(ne) this for anyone with the *same, specific* problem?" *and* "Is this plan reasonable, feasible and appropriate for the trainee and this department?" If yes, write a specific plan of action (SJM Remedial Training Worksheet), implement the plan and see if there is improvement. If *any* improvement is observed, this and all feedback should be noted and shared with the trainee. This process may be repeated as necessary as long as the problem continues to be viewed as remediable and training remains feasible.

Another common misconception regarding extensions is that there needs to be set duration for it. Reasons often cited for this are concerns over consistency. While consistency is a key to the success of this program for all trainees, with regard to extensions, obtaining it is very simple. Remember the question, "Would the department, or has it in the past, do(ne) this for anyone with the *same, specific* problem?" Maintaining consistency merely requires that you offer the same training opportunities, and duration, for trainees with the *same, specific* problem. Therefore, the need for proper, *specific* problem identification cannot be overemphasized, both for the trainee to discern what performance to improve and the department to remain consistent. Shorter extensions seem to work best in that, if the plan is working but needs more time, another Worksheet can be used. However, if the plan is not working, the agency proactively avoids, for consistency, offering a lengthy plan to this or any other trainee with the *same, specific* problem.

Item 12: Deployment Status of Trainee

In the PTO case study from Savannah, Georgia, under Implementation Experiences, "PTOs enjoyed the flexibility of allowing trainees time to return to the station to complete program assignments while the PTO still answered calls for service."[22]

Contrasting from the PTO model which has Trainees working on PBLs, journals and NPEs, SJM trainees are rarely, if ever, without their FTOs. There are a number of reasons behind this key element, including the philosophy that 1) there is so much to cover in 14 weeks, 2) so much can happen at any given time (whether an opportunity for self-initiated field activity or calls for service), and mostly 3) the FTO cannot provide feedback on performance if s/he is not there to observe trainee processes.

Item 14: Rotation Between FTOs

Rotation to different FTOs, by phase (and in Phase 1-3), is encouraged 1) so that the trainee derives the benefit of learning from different FTOs and 2) to ensure that FTO feedback remains valid (standardized) and reliable (consistent). In contrast to this, for Phase 4, the quasi-solo evaluation only experience, it is recommended that trainees rotate back to a previous phase's FTO, eliminating the need for the trainee to adjust to another new "training" environment. Regardless of phase, all FTOs should be consistent in their application of the evaluation process. Ex.: given a specific example of a job-related performance which would warrant a rating of "4" in Phase 1, it would similarly warrant that same rating in Phase 4.

Item 16: Rating Frequency

Again, the SJM is based on JTA data used to develop SEGs. These standards clearly articulate to trainees the expectations for achieving success on the street and, accordingly, in the program. Trainees receive frequent and ongoing feedback as to their progress toward that end, beginning with Daily Observation Reports (DORs). These detail progress toward job-related performance, on a scale of 1 to 7, on 30-35 specific categories (depending on user agency needs and the frequency of the tasks).

The proven and still effective technique of successive approximation[23] is used especially for complex tasks, such that the trainee receives feedback after each step of the task, rather than expecting him/her to get it completely right, the first time, all at once, before receiving feedback. In this way, trainees can discern what step(s) has been completed correctly and what step(s) needs performance correction to complete the task, in its entirety, successfully. Accordingly, the SJM sets trainees up to succeed, *not* fail. While mistakes can, and are, made by the trainee, embarrassment, a questionable training technique, is minimized by the self confidence gained through the use of successive approximations, experiential learning activities (ELAs), and feedback.

The FTO continually provides the trainee with opportunities to learn, through actual field experiences, call debriefings and ELAs, allowing the trainee to self-discover viable options. In doing so, trainees are equipped with a solid foundation from which to draw upon for any future situations they might encounter.

Item 17: Evaluation Only Phase

In Phase 4 of the SJM, the trainee is expected to function as a "quasi-solo" officer. The FTO is always still with the trainee, inquiring as to trainee thought process, observing, asking about alternatives, providing feedback, and answering questions if needed. However, the trainee is encouraged to use the successes and resources they have acquired to date to problem solve for themselves. Trainees experience reinforcement of the continual need and process of exploring, gathering and utilizing resources available to them and the benefits of lifelong learning.

Item 18: Functional Termination Authority

One of the biggest challenges FTOs face is having their recommendations second guessed by those outside the program. Using the SJM, by the time an FTO must decide to recommend termination, the decision is *not* based solely on that FTO's perceptions. Rather, it is objectively based using trainee input; the SEGs; DORs; remedial training strategies; and input from other FTOs, Field Training Sergeants (FTS), the Field Training Officer Coordinator (FTOC), Bi-Weekly Meetings, and, where applicable, other experts consulted as to the deficiency(ies). Any departmental personnel in the chain of command subject to receiving an FTO Program recommendation for termination packet should be completely versed in the SJM, it's historical and present use in said department, and the organization's termination process.

Additional Considerations

PBL Exercise #1: Non-Emergency Incident Response[24]

Vehicle Stop

You and your partner stop a car on a busy street with a great deal of pedestrian and vehicular traffic. You have stopped the car for speeding in a school zone. Upon stopping the vehicle you notice the passengers in the rear seats strapping on their seatbelts. As you approach the vehicle, you note the windows are down and you hear agitated voices. All occupants of the vehicle are from the same minority ethnic group. The passenger in the front seat complains loudly to the others about racial profiling. At this point he has not yet seen you. Several passers-by have stopped to watch the event. Upon request, the driver produces identification, but the passengers are argumentative and refuse to identify themselves.

You must present to your Police Training Officer two or more possible outcomes for this Problem-Based Learning Exercise. In each instance you must include the following:

Ideas — Record initial responses to the problem. What are two separate possible ways you can deal with this situation? Explain them to your PTO.
• What are your initial thoughts on solving this problem?
• What are the issues?

Facts—List all of the known facts about the problem. For example, you are in a school zone; the passengers in the vehicle will not provide identification.

• What do you know?

Learning Issues—Identify the relevant content from the learning matrix for each decision. For example, what do you know about racial profiling and what conflict resolution skills are most appropriate in this circumstance?

• What do you need to know to solve this problem?

• Where can you find it?

• Whom should you contact?

• What resources are available to solve this problem?

• What other information do you need?

Action Plans—Create a precise and specific plan for either solving or reducing the problem. Your action plan should arise from what you know about the problem and what your research has taught you. For example, once you speak to a variety of individuals and carry out your research during the "learning issues phase," what plan can you now develop, using the new information you have, to help you deal effectively with this problem?

• What can you do to solve or reduce this problem?

• Do you make arrests?

• Describe the rationale for each decision.

• Describe the possible consequences of each decision in your action plan.

• Describe how you would behave given each set of circumstances.

Remember, this is an ill-structured problem, and your action plan does not have a simple solution.

Aside from the previously mentioned need for solution / expectation parameters, i.e. some type of written expectation for successful completion of the problem based learning (PBL), this particular scenario as a PBL is worth noting.

As well, the SJM would expect the FTO to cover this type of incident with the assigned Trainee, however the training method would be very different. FTOs are encouraged to use experiential learning activities (ELAs) such as "what if" scenarios, role plays, demonstrations, case studies, observation, debate, or simulation, as appropriate, to augment that which they are responsible for ensuring the trainee learns (ex.: from the SEGs and Trainee Task List). This type of methodology allows the trainee to discover for him/herself the applicable knowledge, skills and attitudes (KSAs), while deploying a practical problem solving model such as SARA (Scanning, Analysis, Response, Assessment).

Trainees practice the real life skill of problem solving quickly, when needed for officer safety reasons, without the expectation of using a complex model. Is there a potential that the expected use of the PBL problem solving process, exampled in the above exercise, might cause a false sense of dependency on in-depth analysis? FTOs have already seen where some trainees are not making decisions. Whether they are unwilling, unknowing, uncertain, reluctant to make a mistake, or for a variety of other reasons which should be explored with the trainee, the reality is that a decision needs to be made, and sometime without the luxury of in-depth analysis.

<u>CA POST's Police Training Program (PTP)</u>

The California Commission on Peace Officer Standards and Training (CA POST), reports that The Police Training Program (PTP) was designed in 1999, as an alternative to the Field Training Program (FTP) model, through a grant funded by the Department of Justice Office of Community Policing Services (COPS). California approved the PTP as an alternate training method in 2007. The PTP employs current adult learning theory, particularly Problem-Based Learning, as the primary method of instruction. Using phased training (called Substantive Topic Phases), Journaling as a learning tool, and focusing on Core Competencies, the PTP is intended to develop problem-solving skills and engage peace officers in the communities they serve.[25]

Four of the significant ways in which the PTP seems to vary from the PTO, yet resemble the SJM, are the inclusion of:

1. *Rubric Assessment for Neighborhood Portfolio Exercise* (NPE), adapted from a document produced by the Richmond Police Department[26], and presumably used to evaluate trainee success with the assignment as it notes:

> "Receiving a "Not Achieved" mark in any area of the NPE assessment will result in a failing evaluation mark for the assignment."

The necessity for adding this document, by both at large state POST and a PTO "pilot site"[27] reinforces this author's aforementioned concern for providing "some type of written expectation for successful completion of the PBL" as "...Policing does have acceptable rights and wrongs leading to potentially risky consequences / outcomes..." (see above: Changes to the SJM: Adult Learning and PBL Exercise #1)

2. *Prescriptive Training Report*, the sample of which uses the terms "scenario training" and "simulation".[28]

The comments for use of prescriptive training and its accompanying report form have many similarities to the SJM remedial training protocol and its accompanying Remedial Training Worksheet.[29]

3. POST's *Minimum Content Areas for Training Manuals* document which cautions: "IMPORTANT: PTP Supervisors/Administrators/Coordinators (PTP SACs) MUST ENSURE that the following required content is delivered to trainees throughout the agency's training program, and that trainees sufficiently demonstrate an understanding and/or practical application of the subject matter."[30]

Although formatting of the document varies greatly from the SJM Trainee Task List, its purpose is clearly similar in that it verifies, standardizes, and lists specific job-related tasks which *must* be accomplished and not left to chance. (see above: Comparative Analysis chart, Item #8).

In another example of this similarity, the PTP's Core Competency Performance Outcomes[31] multipage document does, in fact, closely resemble the SJM Trainee Task List as do its instructions for use.[32] In the COPS report analyzing Case Studies, one of their initial "pilot site" departments, Lowell, Massachusetts also recognized the need for this traditional training component.[33]

4. Police Training Program (PTP) Completion Record / Competency Attestation, wherein the trainee, Primary PTO, and agency head must attest to the trainee having "performed competently in all performance outcomes"[34].

Yet again, the PTP provides support of the aforementioned SJM emphasis of the need for documentation of *all* training, not just critical or other incidents selected for noting in journals, "which are not part of the evaluation process"[35] and/or Coaching and Training Reports (CTRs).

These four examples from the CA POST PTP, all of which closely resemble Key Elements of the SJM, provide strong evidence that the latter is not as behind the times and in dire need of replacement as repeatedly implied in both the aforementioned COPS documents or the President's Task Force on 21st Century Policing, 2015. Rather, the SJM simply does not espouse to the virtues of PBLs for use in field training, a philosophical and justifiable difference. As such, the SJM is not wrong; unchanged; inflexible; failing to be "based on current research knowledge of adult learning modalities"; nor "in many ways it even conflicts with innovative training strategies that...support organizational procedural justice"; but rather, just different.

Perpetual Bias

Maybe it *is* time for change, but the rationale cited for doing so, by proponents of the PTO model, are based on ill-conceived, false premises and inaccurate information. Research efforts to determine the source of this perpetual bias revealed the following data.

COPS / PERF PTO Model

An article written by Jerry Hoover, both a core member of the original COPS / PERF PTO model development team and the project director / design team leader for the Reno Project, stated:

> "The Reno Model was never meant to replace the San Jose Model. Admittedly, some of the design team who were primarily academics did not like the San Jose Model and attacked it in their writings. This is unfortunate because it did not represent the beliefs of the practitioners, who believed that the San Jose Model was an important innovation in police training and that the Reno Model is an evolutionary extension of that innovation. The San Jose Model will always have a place in police training, but it is not for everyone."[36]

President's Task Force

Written in 2015, this document's findings also showed a predisposition *against* the SJM and *toward* use of the PTO. An examination as to the composition of the Task Force's members and their various backgrounds determined:

> "The Task Force will include, among others, law enforcement representatives and community leaders and will operate in collaboration with Ron Davis, Director of DOJ's Community Oriented Policing Services (COPS) Office. The Task Force will build on the extensive research currently being conducted by COPS;"[37] Mr. Davis' role was as Executive Director of the Task Force.[38]

> Of the 11 remaining members of the Task Force, 3 had direct ties to, and relationships, with the COPS Office / Programs.[39]

> Of the remaining 11 members of the Task Force, 5 were active members of PERF, one of whom served as a co-chair for the Task Force while simultaneously serving as the PERF President.[40]

> More than 30 PERF members testified before the Task Force during public hearings.[41]

> Training and Education was one of the 6 pillars for which Listening Sessions were held, wherein interested parties were invited to submit input and recommendations (testify). A review of this session's testimony showed *only* one mention of field training, and nothing regarding either the SJM or PTO models:

> **"Recommendation #4:** ...In addition to the training of police officers in basic academy course **we need to train field training officers,**...to ensure officers are going to work in 21st century police agencies... **We need field training officers who understand what will be required to police in the 21st century, and their role in training officers to fill that role.**"[42] [emphasis added]

This data reveals that, 6 of the 12 Task Force members, or 50%, had a direct connection with the entities responsible for developing the PTO model. As such, the notion that members may have been predisposed or susceptible to preconceived opinions about both models is not far fetched.

Conclusion

If change *is* truly needed, and not just for the sake of pursuing the latest innovation in lieu of addressing problems inherent to the agency regardless of what innovation is implemented, then perhaps it needs to be in the form of correcting misapplications of the *still* viable, effective and progressive SJM.

The differences between the SJM FTO and the PTO models are not a lack of change, liability protection, inflexibility nor failing to embrace community oriented policing, but rather philosophical difference between training and evaluation. The SJM places emphasis on and embraces the use of ELAs and specific, job-related, objective performance feedback. This difference, both now and historically, allows the trainee to practice and gain real life skills while simultaneously receiving continual feedback as to how they are progressing toward expectations.

Conversely, the PTO places emphasis on and embraces PBLs and critical incident feedback / discussions.

For this author, having been in the position of, and advising various other FTOC's, preparing Termination Packets, the decision for the success of the trainee and the department was both certain and evident using the San Jose Model.

[1] The Police Society for Problem Based Learning, *PTO*, http://www.pspbl.org/pto, (accessed September 24, 2015).

[2] President's Task Force on 21st Century Policing, 2015, *Final Report of the President's Task Force on 21st Century Policing*, p. 60, Washington, DC: Office of Community Oriented Policing Services, published 2015.

[3] Community Oriented Policing Services, Community Oriented Policing Services, U.S. Department of Justice, *PTO: An Overview and Introduction*, p. 4, http://www.cops.usdoj.gov/files/ric/Publications/CaseStudiesPDF3.pdf (accessed September 24, 2015).

[4] Community Oriented Policing Services, U.S. Department of Justice, *Police Training Officer (PTO) Manual*, preface, Product ID: COPS-W0358, June 6, 2004, http://ric-zai-inc.com/Publications/cops-w0358-pub.pdf, (accessed September 24, 2015).

[5] Kaminsky, Glenn F., *The Field Training Concept in Criminal Justice Agencies*, p. xiv, Upper Saddle River, N.J.: Prentice Hall, 2001.

[6] Pitts, Steven, Glensor, Ronald W., Peak, Kenneth J., *The Police Training Officer (PTO) Program: A Contemporary Approach to Postacademy Recruit Training*, The Police Chief, Vol. 74, No. 8, Alexandria, VA, August 2007.

[7] Community Oriented Policing Services, *Police Training Officer (PTO) Manual*, preface.

[8] Ibid., preface.

[9] President's Task Force on 21st Century Policing, 2015, *Final Report of the President's Task Force on 21st Century Policing*, p. 60, Washington, DC: Office of Community Oriented Policing Services, published 2015.

[10] Community Oriented Policing Services, *PTO: An Overview and Introduction*, p. 31, 33, 37.

[11] Jerry Hoover, The Reno Model Police Training Officer (PTO) Program, NAFTO News, p. 17, December 2004.

[12] Ibid.

[13] Greenberg, Jerald, *A Taxonomy of Organizational Justice Theories*, Academy of Management Review, Vol. 12, No. 1, p. 9–22, Ohio State University, 1987.

[14] Leventhal, G. S., *What should be done with equity theory? New approaches to the study of fairness in social relationship*, in K. Gergen, M. Greenberg, & R. Willis (Eds.), Social exchange: Advances in theory and research, p. 27–55, New York: Plenum Press, 1980.

[15] Folger, R., & Greenberg, J., *Procedural Justice; An interpretative analysis of personnel systems*, in K. Rowlands & G. Ferris (Eds.), Research in personnel and human resources management, Vol. 3 p. 141-183, Greenwich, CT: JAI Press, 1985.

[16] Community Oriented Policing Services, *PTO: An Overview and Introduction*, p. 34, 39, 40; *and* Community Oriented Policing Services, *Police Training Officer (PTO) Manual*, preface, p. 31, 156.

[17] President's Task Force on 21st Century Policing, 2015, p. 60.

[18] Kaminsky, Glenn F., p. 11.

[19] Kaminsky, Glenn F., p. 10-23.

[20] Community Oriented Policing Services, *Police Training Officer (PTO) Manual*, p. 156-157.

[21] Kaminsky, Glenn F., p. 21.

[22] Community Oriented Policing Services, *PTO: An Overview and Introduction*, p. 24.

[23] Skinner, B.F., *Science and human behavior*, p. 92–3, Oxford, England: Macmillan, 1953.

[24] Community Oriented Policing Services, *Police Training Officer (PTO) Manual*, p. 53.

[25] California Commission on Peace Officer Standards and Training, Police Training Program Guide, Police Training Officer, Problem-Based Learning Model, Vol. 1: Overview & Appendices, p. v, September 2014.

[26] Ibid., app. D, p. A-17.

[27] Community Oriented Policing Services, *PTO: An Overview and Introduction*, p. 6.

[28] California Commission on Peace Officer Standards and Training, app. E, p. A-21-23.

[29] Ibid., p. 2-12.

[30] Ibid., app. H, p. A-41-42.

[31] California Commission on Peace Officer Standards and Training, *Police Training Program Guide, Police Training Officer, Problem-Based Learning Model, Vol. 2: Training Workbook - All Phases*, p. 12-26, 33-47, 54-68, 75-89, September 2014.

[32] Ibid., p. 12-26, 33-47, 54-68, 75-89, September 2014.

[33] Community Oriented Policing Services, *PTO: An Overview and Introduction*, p. 27.

[34] California Commission on Peace Officer Standards and Training, *Police Training Program Guide, Police Training Officer, Problem-Based Learning Model, Vol. 1: Overview & Appendices*, app. I, p. A-43, September 2014.

[35] Community Oriented Policing Services, *Police Training Officer (PTO) Manual*, p 27.

[36] Jerry Hoover.

[37] *The White House Fact Sheet: Strengthening Community Policing*, The White House, Office of the Press Secretary, December 01, 2014, https://www.whitehouse.gov/the-press-office/2014/12/01/fact-sheet-strengthening-community-policing (accessed on September 26, 2015).

[38] Subject to Debate, a newsletter of the Police Executive Research Forum, *PERF Members Testify Before President's Task Force on 21st Century Policing, President Obama released the Final Report of his Task Force on 21st Century Policing on May 18*, Vol. 29, No. 2, March/April/May 2015, http://www.policeforum.org/assets/docs/Subject_to_Debate /Debate2015/debate_2015_marmay.pdf (accessed September 26, 2015).

[39] Office of Community Oriented Policing Services, Community Policing: Leading the Way to a Safer Nation Conference, July 27-29, 2006, Washington, D.C., http://www.cops.usdoj.gov/pdf/conference/Conf_Prog_FINAL_P1.pdf (accessed September 26, 2015), *and* Testimony of Dr. Cedric Alexander, National President of the National Organization of Black Law Enforcement Executives (NOBLE) Before the Senate Judiciary Committee Subcommittee on the Constitution, Civil Rights and Human Rights Hearing on "The State of Civil and Human Rights in the United States" December 9, 2014, p.5, http://www.noblenational.org/Cedric%20 Alexander%20Senate%20Testimony.pdf (accessed September 26, 2015), *and* Community Policing Dispatch, The e-newsletter of the COPS Office | Volume 4 | Issue 9 | September 2011, *COPS Conference Recap, August 2011*, http://cops.usdoj.gov/html/dispatch/09-2011/COPSConfRecap.asp (accessed September 26, 2015).

[40] Subject to Debate, a newsletter of the Police Executive Research Forum, *PERF Members Testify Before President's Task Force on 21st Century Policing, President Obama released the Final Report of his Task Force on 21st Century Policing on May 18*.

[41] Ibid.

[42] Testimony before the President's Task Force on 21st Century Policing, Listening Session 5: Training and Education, Phoenix, AZ, February 14, 2015, Winegar, Steven, Ph.D. *Training Officers to Police in the 21st Century*, p. 101, http://www.cops.usdoj.gov/pdf/taskforce/02-14-2015/Invited_Testimony_February_14.pdf (accessed September 26, 2015).

84957794R00031